An Easy-to-sing, Easy-to-stage Christmas Musical for Children
Created and Compiled by Kimberly Meiste

Contents

PUBLISHING COMPANY

lillenas.com

(At the beginning of the musical, some children have already arrived at the party, but ANN, TYLER, JAKE, and other children may enter with coats and boots like they are just arriving.)

Gloria!

CARTER ROBERTSON

CARTER ROBERTSON
and Traditional English Melody
Arr. by Barny Robertson

CD: 2 / 3 *1st / 2nd time*
CD: 28 / 29 *1st / 2nd time*

Glo - ri - a! We are sing - ing Glo - ri - a! 1. We're
2. To -

on our way to share the news of Je - sus' birth, of Je - sus' birth. We're
day the Sav - ior has been born in Beth - le - hem, in Beth - le - hem. To -

on our way to share the news of Je - sus' birth with the shep - herds.
day the Sav - ior has been born in Beth - le - hem in Ju - de - a!

4

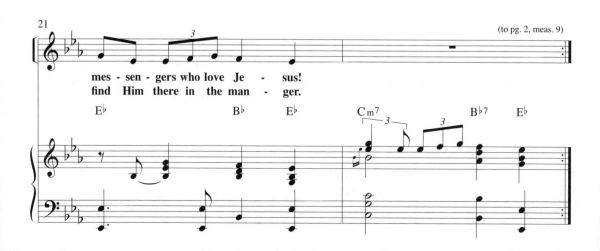

(As the song ends, all the children high-five one another and laugh. Groups break off and mingle. ANN *walks up to* JAKE *and* TYLER.*)*

ANN: Merry Christmas, guys!

JAKE and TYLER: Merry Christmas, Ann!

ANN: It's pretty neat that we get to have a Christmas party today.

TYLER: And we don't have to go to Sunday School! *(Laughs really loudly and elbows* JAKE, *who is surprised and stumbles back)*

ANN: You guys are so weird! Anyways, have you seen Kristy? I didn't get to see her after the musical last week because all of her family was here.

JAKE: Yeah, they were making her take pictures up on the set afterwards!

TYLER: Talk about weird!

ANN: Well I think it was pretty cool for her grandparents to come all the way from up north!

(As ANN *is speaking,* KRISTY *walks in with her new neighbor,* LAURA. *Both girls are carrying presents.)*

KRISTY *(laughingly)*: Are you guys talking about me?

*(*TYLER *and* JAKE *are taken aback, not sure if* KRISTY *is joking or not.)*

JAKE *(awkwardly)*: No way, Kristy. We would never . . .

TYLER *(interrupting)*: Yeah, we were only . . .

ANN: Why don't you guys go get some punch or something!

JAKE *(nervously)*: That's a great idea! C'mon Tyler! *(Grabs* TYLER'S *arm and they run up SR.)*

*(*KRISTY *puts down her present and hugs* ANN. *Meanwhile,* LAURA *is standing close to* KRISTY, *obviously nervous.)*

ANN: I didn't get to see you last week after the show!

KRISTY: I know! My parents took a million pictures and then my grandparents took the whole family out for lunch.

ANN: Wow, where did you go?

KRISTY *(talking really fast)*: Well first my grandpa wanted to go to that buffet place. Gross! The only good part about that place is the ice cream! Then, my mom suggested the one with the indoor playground on Main Street. Then I said, "Mom! I'm not five anymore!" Then my dad . . .

LAURA *(clears throat, timidly)*: Where do I put my present?

KRISTY *(still speaking rather quickly)*: I'm so sorry, Laura! I'd like you to meet my best friend Ann. Annie, this is my new neighbor Laura. She just moved in two weeks ago. I was so busy before the musical, that I didn't get the chance to invite her to come, but I figured the party today would be a great time for her to meet everybody and then maybe her parents could come next time . . .

ANN *(interrupting)*: Kristy! Slow down! I know you're in the Christmas spirit, but I think you're scaring Laura.

(They all laugh. LAURA *finally smiles and looks more comfortable.)*

ANN: The presents go under the tree over there in the corner.

*(*LAURA *and* KRISTY *walk over to the tree)*

MR. BELL *(trying to get everyone's attention)*: OK, class! You guys did such an excellent job last Sunday. I heard a lot of great comments from your families and many others. As we have our party today, we are going to sing some of our favorite songs from the musical. Who's ready for the first song?

JAKE *(calling out from the punch table)*: How about "I Will Sing Songs of Joy?" That was my favorite!

MR. BELL: Nice suggestion, Jake. Let me get the CD ready!

*(*MR. BELL *walks over to the CD player to start the next track. The children gather together at the front of the class to sing.* LAURA *stays back by the Christmas tree and watches because she doesn't know the songs from the musical. You could place a chair for her to sit in as well.)*

(Music begins)

I Will Sing Songs of Joy

Adapted from Psalms

CRYSTAL DAVIS CLAY

PLEASE NOTE: Copying of this product is NOT covered by CCLI licenses. For CCLI information call 1-800-234-2446.

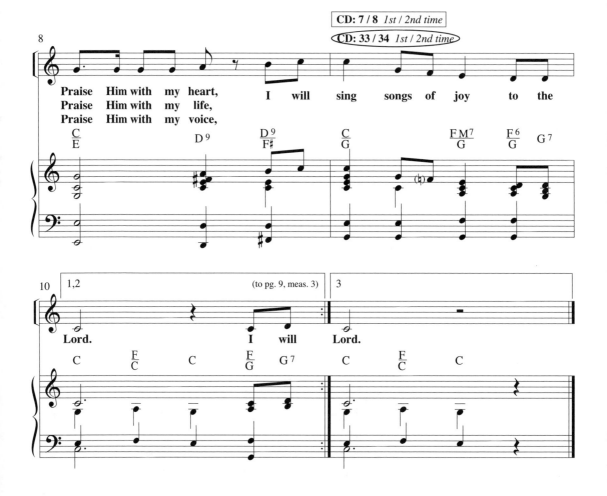

MR. BELL: Great job, kids! Jake, what was your favorite part of that song?

JAKE: I guess the part that talks about how we can praise Jesus in different ways. Plus, I love to sing that song at the top of my lungs!

MR. BELL: Nice. Thanks for sharing, Jake. Alright, make sure everyone makes it to the craft table today. We're decorating ornaments for our Christmas tree.

(The class breaks apart and "mingles" again. ANN, LAURA, and JAKE meet CS.)

JAKE *(to LAURA)*: So, who are you?

ANN: This is Laura, Kristy's new neighbor. She just moved from . . . you know what? I don't know where you moved from!

LAURA *(as she speaks, she begins to let out some frustration little by little)*: I actually moved from Florida. My family and I had to move because of a hurricane. First we lived with my grandparents, but now we're living with my aunt up here for awhile.

JAKE: Whoa, wait a minute. Did you lose your house and everything? I saw stories about that on the news!

LAURA: Yup. It was scary. We had to move fast and we also had to leave a lot of stuff behind . . . and you know what else?

JAKE: What?

LAURA: I had never seen snow before two weeks ago!

ANN: Wow, Laura. That's crazy! You've had a lot of new stuff to get used to.

(KRISTY *runs up to talk to* LAURA.)

KRISTY: Laura! I want you to come meet Mr. Bell. He's the nicest teacher ever!

LAURA: OK, Kristy. *(To* ANN *and* JAKE*)* I guess I'll see you guys later! *(Runs off with* KRISTY*)*

ANN *(still stunned)*: Wow, Jake. That's crazy!

JAKE: I know! I'm sure Laura's Christmas is going to be really different.

ANN: It's great that Kristy brought her to the party, but I wish she could have come to see the musical last week.

JAKE: I don't know . . .the musical was all about joy and I'm sure Laura hasn't been too happy lately . . .

MR. BELL *(as he makes his way up to the front)*: OK, kids! Can I have your attention? Let's sing another song!

TYLER *(from the crafts table, jumping up and down)*: Ooo! Ooo! Can I request my favorite song this time?

MR. BELL: Sure, Tyler. Which song?

TYLER: I loved "Go, Tell It on the Mountain" because I could dance to it! *(Breaks out in a crazy dance, which makes everyone laugh)*

MR. BELL: That is some impressive action there, Tyler, but let's not try to break any bones, OK? Hey, does anybody remember the memory verse that went with this song?

KRISTY: I do, Mr. Bell! It was Luke 1:14.

MR. BELL: Great, Kristy! Let's all say the verse together.

ALL: "He will be a joy and delight to you, and many will rejoice because of his birth.

MR. BELL: Awesome! Now let me get that CD going, OK!

(MR. BELL *walks over to the CD player to start the next track. The children gather together at the front of the class to sing.* LAURA *actually tries to sing this with the children, as it is a more familiar Christmas carol. She doesn't know all the words though, and the audience can see her struggle in various places. Music begins)*

Go, Tell It on the Mountain

JOHN W. WORK, JR.

Afro-American Spiritual
Arr. by Peter Jacobs

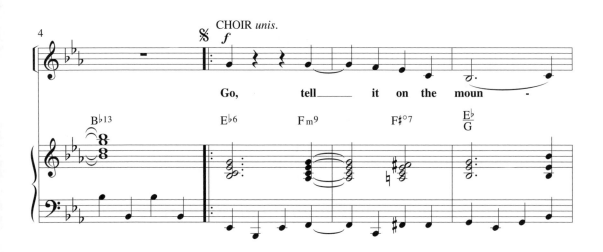

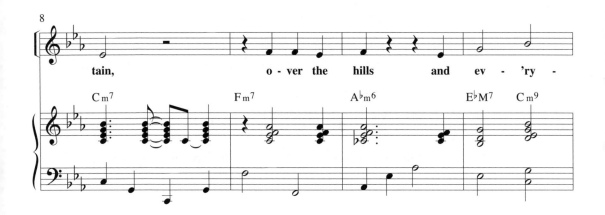

SOLO 2

f

He came to bring us free-dom that cold De- cem - ber night,

And if we but re- ceive Him we'll walk in God's pure

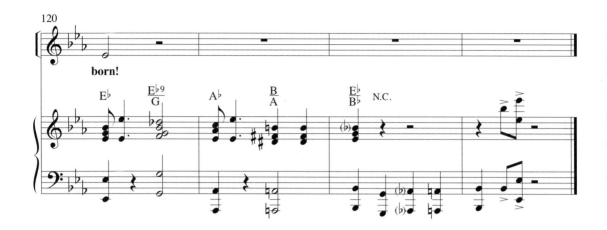

(Everyone scatters once again, moving to different table and mingling groups. TYLER breaks out dancing again, causing JAKE to join in with him this time. ANN, KRISTY, and LAURA watch in amusement.)

TYLER: Oh yeah! Break it down!

JAKE *(stops dancing)*: You broke what?

(The girls erupt in laughter.)

TYLER: C'mon Jake. Let's go show Andrew our moves!

(They move up to the food table area)

ANN: So Laura, are you going to start school with us after Christmas break? Kristy and I have the same teacher, Mr. Woodruff, and it would be so cool if you were in the same class as us!

LAURA: Well, I don't know actually. We might move again if my dad finds a job somewhere else.

KRISTY: I hope you don't move. We were just getting to know you, and we need another girl around with Tyler and Jake! *(Jokingly)* We can't handle them on our own!

ANN: Yeah, and we need another person for our quizzing team too!

LAURA: That sounds like fun! *(All of a sudden downcast)* I don't know though . . .

TYLER *(runs up with a present from under the tree)*: Hmm, I wonder what's in here?
       (Starts to shake the present)

ANN: Tyler, you better stop! You could break whatever's inside!

MR. BELL *(from the crafts table)*: I need everyone who hasn't made an ornament to quickly make one, please. Finish them up so I can take a picture with all of you in front of the tree later!

KRISTY *(to* LAURA*)*: Oh no! We haven't made ours yet. Let's go!

(They both move up CS to the craft table.)

TYLER: Who's the girl with Kristy?

ANN: That's Laura. Her family is going through a really hard time.

TYLER: What do you mean?

ANN: They were in Florida when the hurricane hit! They had to move up here with her aunt. And her dad can't find a job!

TYLER: I saw that hurricane on TV.

ANN: I just wish that we could cheer her up.

TYLER: My dancing might cheer her up. *(Does a quick funny move and they start laughing together.)*

MR. BELL: OK, everybody! It's time for another song! Hey, why don't we put our ornaments on the tree while we sing? I think a great song for this would be "Rejoice!," don't you?

ALL: Yeah! Cool!

(Music begins)

(During the song, the children move in a line to place their ornaments on the tree. Be sure to avoid traffic jams and try to always have one small group of children singing towards the audience. LAURA *remains at the craft table working on her ornament during the song. She finishes near the end of the song and is the last one to place her ornament on the tree.)*

Rejoice!

LINDA REBUCK

DAVID HUNTSINGER
Arr. by Joseph Linn

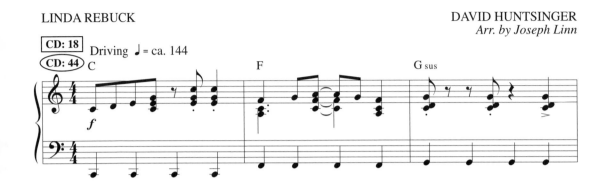

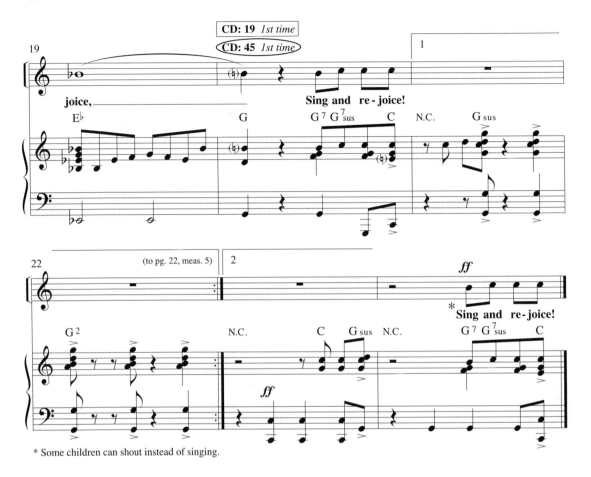

* Some children can shout instead of singing.

(As the song ends, everybody moves back to their small groups. There can now be a group of children playing a game or a group stringing popcorn for the tree. ANN, KRISTY, LAURA, *and* TYLER *are all DS center.)*

LAURA: That was a great song, guys. I bet your musical got a standing ovation!

TYLER *(dusts off his shoulders)*: Well, we don't want to brag, but . . .

KRISTY *(interjecting)*: Ann did the best job in the musical. She was the last to bow in the curtain call at the end. If anyone deserved a standing ovation, it was Ann!

ANN: Aw, thanks Kristy! It was hard to memorize everything, but the performance was great and I only messed up two lines!

JAKE *(running up with a plate of food)*: You guys! I have never tasted something this amazing in my whole entire life!

KRISTY: What are you talking about?

JAKE: It's these cookies! They taste like elves made them . . . better yet, Mrs. Claus!

TYLER: Let me try! *(Grabs one off the plate and puts the whole cookie in his mouth. Begins to speak with his mouth full, pieces of cookie flying out.)* Yum! Yow wight! Theeth awe amathing!

ANN: Gross, Tyler! Say it, don't spray it!

(JAKE puts a whole cookie in his mouth too, all to copy Tyler.)

KRISTY: Ew! *(All of a sudden in a sweet voice)* Why don't you go let Andrew taste the cookies too?

TYLER: Good idea! *(Overdramatically like a superhero)* Quick, before they're all gone!

(Both TYLER and JAKE bound away)

LAURA *(obviously more cheerful)*: I can see why you guys need another girl around here, that's for sure!

ANN *(noticing the small change with LAURA)*: This is nothing! Wait 'til the Easter musical! *(Puts her arm around LAURA)* One time the boys had to dress up like sheep and they wouldn't stop saying, "Baa, Baa" for weeks!

LAURA *(trying to hold back some laughter)*: That sounds really funny!

MR. BELL: Alright guys and gals, who's ready to sing again? We still have a couple more songs from the musical. Two of my favorites are the carols "Away in a Manger" and "Silent Night."

LAURA *(surprised)*: Hey, I know those songs!

MR. BELL: Well then, you can sing along with us Laura! Let's re-create the nativity scene we did! Ann, why don't you start us off with the verse you recited?

(As ANN begins reciting the verse, everybody scurries over the stage finding shepherd staffs and wise men gifts. KRISTY finds the baby Jesus doll and hands it to LAURA. She is pleased to find that this gift of joy has landed right in her lap. A full explanation and diagram of the nativity scene can be found in the Production Notes on page 40.)

ANN: "An angel of the Lord appeared to them, and the glory of the Lord shone around them, and they were terrified. But the angel said to them, 'Do not be afraid. I bring you good news of joy that will be for all the people. *(Music begins)* Today in the town of David a Savior has been born to you; he is Christ the Lord. This will be a sign to you: You will find the baby wrapped in cloths and lying in a manger.'"

Away in a Manger

with

Silent Night! Holy Night!

Anonymous and
JOHN THOMAS MCFARLAND

JAMES R. MURRAY
Arr. by Dennis Allen

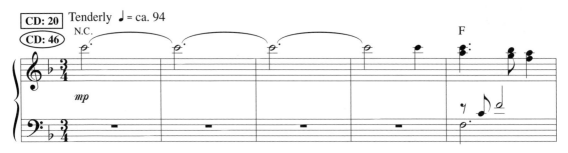

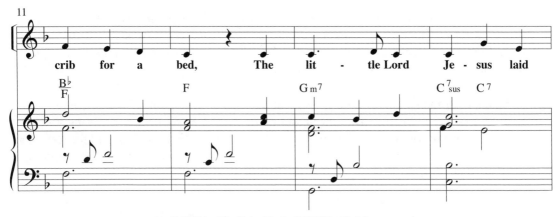

down His sweet head. The stars in the sky_____ looked

down where He lay, The lit - tle Lord Je - sus a -

CD: 21
CD: 47

sleep on the hay.

Be near me, Lord Je - sus; I ask Thee to

CD: 22
CD: 48

*"Silent Night! Holy Night!"

*Words by JOSEPH MOHR; Music by FRANZ GRUBER.

30

(As the children start to branch off again, MR. BELL *pulls* LAURA *aside.* TYLER *and* JAKE *grab their coats and boots and run offstage.)*

MR. BELL: Laura, I wondered if I could speak to you for a moment?

LAURA *(uneasy at first)*: Um, OK. Sure.

MR. BELL: Well, Kristy's parents told me about your family situation. I just wanted to let you know that our Sunday School class is going to be praying that your dad finds a job. I'm guessing that Christmas is going to be hard for you this year, but I believe God's watching out for your family.

LAURA: Thanks. It's hard to get used to Christmas like this. Everything's different here. Even the weather.

MR. BELL *(trying to get her to smile)*: Yeah, but up here you can go ice-skating outside! You can drink your hot chocolate so fast that you burn your tongue! You can go sledding and build snowmen!

LAURA: That all sound great! I'll have to give those a shot!

MR. BELL *(laughing)*: That's the spirit!

LAURA: I'll tell you what, Mr. Bell. I think I'm going to go home and try to cheer up my parents with my ornament and a Christmas cookie. My mom will like the ornament, and I know that my dad will LOVE the cookie!

MR. BELL: You deserve a gift too. I'd like to give you this Bible, if that's OK. You know, I've learned that sometimes bad things happen to us, Laura, and that's when we've got to turn to Jesus, the source of our true joy.

LAURA: Thanks, Mr. Bell! I lost my Bible in the storm so mom and I have been sharing. You know what, I better get back to Kristy, but can I talk to you later about Sunday School and Bible Quizzing?

MR. BELL: Of course! Anytime!

LAURA: OK, thanks! *(Runs back over to* KRISTY *and* ANN*, who have just finished a conversation with some other girls.)*

KRISTY: There you are, Laura!

LAURA: I was talking with Mr. Bell. You're right; he is a nice teacher!

ANN: Is that your Bible, Laura?

LAURA: Mr. Bell just gave it to me.

KRISTY: There's a bookmark in it. Looks like he marked you a verse.

(LAURA *opens the Bible and begins to read*)

LAURA: "Yet I will rejoice in the Lord, I will be joyful in God my Savior." Habakkuk 3:18

(TYLER *and* JAKE *run in from outside.*)

TYLER: Dude! Those were the best snow angels we've ever made!

JAKE: I know! The snow out there was perfect packing snow! *(To the girls)* It packed so well that I hit Tyler smack in the face with a giant snowball!

TYLER: Um, are you forgetting something, Jake? I hit you with a huge snowball first!

JAKE *(sarcastically)*: That's funny, Tyler. I don't remember that!

MR. BELL: Alright! Everybody listen up! This was an awesome party! I know that your gifts are really going to help some people who need food this holiday. Now before your parents come, why don't we sing the last song from the musical? And, I hope to see all of you in Sunday School next week. Everyone will be happy to know that we are NOT gonna be talking about sheep.

(TYLER *and* JAKE *snicker and high-five each other as everybody else cheers.*)

MR. BELL: Guys, above all else this season, remember that because Jesus came at Christmas, we have every reason to be full of joy!

(MR. BELL *moves over to the CD player and as the music begins, all the children get together at the front to sing.* LAURA *helps* MR. BELL *get all the presents into boxes marked "Food Pantry." Then, both* LAURA *and* MR. BELL *move up to the choir and sing along with the choir from measure 48 to the end.*)

Joyful, Joyful Medley

includes

Joyful, Joyful, We Adore You

Joy to the World

Arr. by Barny Robertson

*"Joyful, Joyful, We Adore You"

*Words by LINDA LEE JOHNSON; Music by LUDWIG VAN BEETHOVEN. Copyright © 1985, and this arr. © 2001 by Lillenas Publishing Company (SESAC) . All rights reserved. Administered by The Copyright Company, PO Box 128139, Nashville, TN 37212-8139.

PLEASE NOTE: Copying of this product is NOT covered by CCLI licenses. For CCLI information call 1-800-234-2446.

36

CD: 25
CD: 51

we a - dore Thee, God of glo - ry, Lord of light.

He rules the world with truth and grace, And

makes the na - tions prove The

52
glo - ries of His righ - teous - ness, And
D♭ G♭/D♭ D♭ D♭ G♭/D♭ D♭
54
won-ders of His love, And won-ders of His love, And
D♭ D♭2 A♭ A°7
56
won - ders, won - ders of His love. And won-ders and
B♭m G♭ D♭/A♭ G♭ D♭/A♭ A♭7 D♭ Fm/C B♭m B♭m7 G♭
CD: 26
CD: 52
59
won - ders of His love.
D♭/F D♭ G♭/D♭ N.C. E♭9 N.C. A♭7 G♭/D♭ N.C.

Optional Curtain Call: During the "Joyful, Joyful, We Adore Thee" portion of the "Joyful, Joyful Medley," all children can grab their coats to get ready to go home from the party. MR. BELL grabs his coat and a box, like he's going to go deliver the presents. Children bow during the first portion of the song and then begin to sing from measure 62 to the end.

Production Notes

Cast

ANN	Played the main character in the Christmas musical
KRISTY	Ann's best friend
TYLER	Ann and Kristy's friend. The comedian of the group.
JAKE	Tyler's best friend
LAURA	Kristy's new neighbor that comes to the Christmas party
MR. BELL	The children's Sunday School teacher and musical director.
	(A female adult may also play this part, as long as pronouns are changed.)
NATIVITY ACTORS	Children who mime the parts of shepherds, wise men, Joseph, cows and sheep.

Setting

Sunday School Christmas party the week after the annual Christmas musical is performed. All the children are dressed in Christmas-themed clothing. There is a small tree with presents and a table with food and punch. Children who are not speaking dialogue are grouped together in various spots around the stage; "mingling" at the party.

Set Diagram

Food Table		Christmas Tree
	Crafts Table	
Solo Mic		Solo Mic
	Main Drama	CD Player

Props

Coats	Boots	Punch Bowl and Cups
Wrapped Presents or Canned Goods	Cookies	Christmas Ornaments
Wise Men Gifts and Crowns	Bible	Shepherd Staffs
Animal Ears (Sheep and Cows)	CD Player	Baby Jesus Doll
Angel Wings and Halos		Large Cardboard Box

Scripture References (NIV)

Yet I will rejoice in the Lord, I will be joyful in God my Savior. Habakkuk 3:18

He will be a joy and delight to you, and many will rejoice because of his birth. Luke 1:14

An angel of the Lord appeared to them, and the glory of the Lord shone around them, and they were terrified. But the angel said to them, "Do not be afraid. I bring you good news of joy that will be for all the people. Today in the town of David a Savior has been born to you; he is Christ the Lord. This will be a sign to you: You will find the baby wrapped in cloths and lying in a manger." Luke 2:9-12

Nativity Scene

To give other children a part in the musical, you could stage a mimed nativity scene during the song "Away in a Manger *with* Silent Night! Holy Night!" This scene can be produced with great detail in props and costumes or staged simply. To stage simply, dress one girl and one boy in biblical clothes and have them play the parts of Mary and Joseph. Give the girl a doll to hold to symbolize baby Jesus. To stage with great detail, you may add a manger, shepherds, wise men, angels, and even children dressed as animals with cow and sheep ears and costumes. Be careful to be mindful of the time it takes to stage this scene, as the song is about 2 minutes and 40 seconds long.

Extras

Please visit our website to download movements and clip art. T-shirt information is also available @ www.lillenaskids.com on the *A Song of Joy* product page.